CITYZEN

CITYZEN

Joseph Somoza

La Alameda Press
Albuquerque

Grateful acknowledgments to the
following magazines, anthology, and
e-zine that first printed some of these poems:

*Blue Mesa Review, Convolvulus, Hammers, Insurance,
Karawane, Lunarosity, Maryland Poetry Review,
90 Poets of the Nineties* (The Seminole Press),
Sin Fronteras Journal, Voces Fronterizas

Cover art :: *Hand Print*
tempera on paper — Cirrelda Beth Bryan

Back Cover art :: *Yard Rake*
sumi-e ink on paper — J.B. Bryan

ISBN :: 1-88809-31-0

La Alameda Press
9636 Guadalupe Trail NW
Albuquerque, New Mexico 87114

Contents

for Jill

SUCH A DAY!

when the dove coo-coos
and the other dove
echoes the coo-coo.
Then the sun beats down
especially on your black, cotton,
long-sleeve shirt
and your back-of-the-neck
emerging there.
What would have been
a sunburn at Lake Michigan
in June is, here,
a pleasant touch,
blue through the branches,
mountain peaks nearby,
the mountains
peaking at the exact right place,
which is where the blue
comes in,
past where the wires go
separate ways.

—for Michael Mandel,
  Las Cruces, February

OFF THE TRACK

Morning, and the mind
grasping at straws,
or is that "loose ends"? Cats,
especially a young, white cat
sitting near me isn't that particular,
or persevering. He knows to
drop it when an itch
distracts him—off the track,
and therefore free to go
where life leads him.

The road leading
down the hill toward Polk street
past the auto-bodies with
men in overalls. That's
where a sea breeze keeps you
young, you keep returning
to the eucalyptus hill in shade
that leads down
the sunny way to mingle
with other people, food
and books, and aspirations.

Because you aren't something different,
as you feel you are. And later,
you feel hunger to belong.
Crowded streets of Chinatown, where
people on the sidewalks rub together
to produce a culture, roots
for making soup, a nourishment
for lonely hearts.

Afternoon now, slant light
rolls across the yard and
quivers on the wall. It's Sunday
but what does that mean
when you can't pretend that
Monday is the start
of something new? It means
it's always Sunday: church bells
to ignore, fellow citizens
picnicking, dreaming, or promenading
in the mall,
the time of your life
to kill, or to fulfill.

Day break

"My quietness has a man in it. . . .
He has several likenesses." —Frank O'Hara

But each morning he starts out
alike, looking out
at green trees growing
to their maturity, and so forth,
or back. Paired butterflies
peregrinate among the soon-to-be
iris flowers, or maybe the wind
is blowing them along another as yet
unmappable destination—
like the pattern of the pinto cat's fur
sneaking over the arbitrary cinderblock boundaries
between one patch of grass
and another, law being the superimposition
on lawn, grass lacking
representation, though there being no great
complaints, the earth's axis continues
tilting toward another summer of
mornings bursting through the locust tree,
forcing him to close kitchen curtains
as he sips coffee with hot milk,
and draw back inside, half immersed
in liquid reflections and half inside shimmering
particles and scintillations.

Day in March

I don't know what day
it is, except it's payday.

Maybe I should've written
that in third person.

He doesn't know
what day it is, either.

The wind
just blows,

flowers glow,
periwinkles,

little purple-violet
winkles.

It's another day
I'm out here,

the wind too, and boughs
swaying in it—

within the town,
thriving, on the move.

Morning Meditation

Twelve-noon, "time
to be hungry", but I'm not
quite yet,
haven't sat
long enough in my lawn chair
in the yard
while Victor (next door) tinkers
compulsively with his jeep,
and Gray, meowing,
pads toward me
for his head & neck rub
that he craves.
We're all, after all, so
deluded
by our drives
(so says my yoga book, and it's difficult
to disagree)
that we confuse
our bodies with our-selves,
those integrating kernels
of essence
that we share with gods. But,
do I want to be a god? That's
the question.
Could I be disloyal
to my body
that has meant so much,
has given me so much
(of pain too, its true,
but, more importantly, of the authentic
feel of being me)?

The lawnchair, meantime,
has stretched its colored bands
sustaining me,
and my stomach, now,
begins to growl upon
this meditation
that has as its destination
the non-
craving state—
state of *nirvana*—
union of the disembodied—
through a gate swinging
out and in.

Six p.m.

Oh great outdoors!
Now you've given up all
your light.
Now the junipers beside the house
must lose
their ever green
until tomorrow morning.
And I, solitary on the couch—
lights out,
front door open wide—
may be accompanied only
by a little
serenade
of:

    tick tock clock,
    rain-drip-ping eaves,
    rattle of refrigerator.

Gloomy Weather

Whatever I may think,
I'm nowhere but right here
where individual grasses are
popping
out of the cracked ground,
their green enthusiasm
changing the flavor of the place
a little more each day.
In a few days, I
may be cheerful as a bird
and excited to want to
visit someone.
I may wear my peacock shirt
that reminds me of an iris,
but a purple iris
looking like a "fallen woman",
therefore bruised, abused.
Don't you hate it
when somebody starts
sounding like that?
They seem suddenly so
translucent,
the way the sky was
for days,
so we sat inside reading
and in the evening having
Graham crackers
with our hot chocolate,
taking breaks punctually
for the 10 o'clock news,
which told us what we

already knew, but pompously,
and the weatherman was wrong again
though we still hoping
for the next day to be
seasonably sunny.

The Coming

And now, here
comes the magnificent
magnum opus that woke up early,
slowly stretched itself awake,
and began
to speak deliberately, unconcerned
about time passing,
deadlines, coming to a close;
in short, time still to come.

Coming in this
premature summer weather,
this springful
of bird twitters, power saws
and pollen-spreading wind
where even the green plastic
Wal-Mart chairs gleam vividly
as patent leather shoes—
if this were the Shirley Temple 30's—
as it is for some,
and we others
can look it up
in the almanac,
repository
of what we used to be
when our parents were we,
and we
floated in the anticipatory ether
Tibetans speak about
and delineate in colors

and geometric patterns (which must
make it true—anything *that*
regular—
idealized
from the irregular stuff
that nature grows
and shrinks).

Coming to stay this time
outside of time,
with its forceful
metaphorical boots on
that it pulls up by its straps—
and walks forward,
or to the side, or sits back down
to speak,
the sitting posture
being more conducive to thought,
some believe,
(as, for example, Odysseus, short-legged
crafty talker), whereas those
of the peripatetic school
would disagree.
But it's the voice, really,
in the proximity of the head,
that breathes itself alive—
with help from the
thoracic muscles, granted,
(and the lift from strong thighs
can't hurt,

          having come from
so far away as to blur

even the origin
of its place names,
Zazamanc,
or Munsalvaesche.)
Though it isn't even
breathing hard. Seeming
utterly at ease.
Could go on forever.

BALANCE

I can appreciate the completely
personal—to the point,
almost, of self-indulgence.

And I can appreciate
the sensible,
objective, non-demonstrative

under the warm sun that is
not, however, sweltering,
and under the blue
with clouds,

in my yard where a breeze may
come along
whenever something out of my control
would like it to,

though I decide
whether I will notice it,
and to jot it down.

Isn't this the perfect
arrangement—as between
yin and yang?
My mother, say,

raging
in the kitchen
against a hateful cousin

and my father, smirking
quietly in the hall.

About Time

Sure it's not
morning! But it's
afternoon!
(I'm glad I didn't say that more
coercively). Both cats
are probably sleeping, either by the yucca
or another warmest place. And I'm
lethargic in this unseasonable warmth
knowing exactly how they feel (I'm part
feline, I think, though I don't
show it when I purr). If it's
afternoon, it means no rush;
shadows; a quiet restlessness
as if people were getting ready to
call it quits, which means
come home, check the refrigerator, lie
or sit in one of several
favorite places
to drink a beer.
Ah, the excuse
to let several moments slowly pass!
And, really, that's what the sun
does all along!

Seasons

For Frank O'Hara, you want to
take your glasses off, he's so
non-academic.
And while you're at it, look
naked
at the roses
and darker pomegranates
on the neighbor's tree.
Just air
separates you,
the sexy way it felt
breathing
when you first quit smoking
and the night
slipped through the screen
into your study, where you
waited, lights out, for a touch
of the extraordinary
in your ordinary—but, you hoped,
transformable—life.
A Chopin nocturne
pearling from a nearby room,
a breeze,
your younger, selfish self
insisting you were alone,
and sad,
and nothing
but that moment mattered—while
from the back
drifted the warm voice
of your wife storytelling
to the children
before bedtime.

GENESIS

You can't imagine
someone doesn't love you,
someone is not thinking about you
this very moment,
as far as someone is concerned
you might as well not
be.

This strikes you
as the absolute self center,
a tiny world
around which all other bodies rotate,
the antithesis of God.

From this beginning
social institutions sprout, religions
that clash and breed identity
from strife. Art is born.
People everywhere build
bookshelves, devote lives to music.
Philanthropists raise monuments
to ancestors.

students attend universities
to hone their critical faculties.
Understanding
seems near at hand. In your own room,
with a book, you find
contentment.

Brief Recess

Ah, not having to explain, I feel so
light!
(Whoops! I said that earlier)—
so "flighty" maybe,
or "delighted".
Anyway, the clouds
glide on, but non-
linearly. And they transform
but not into any morphs
anthropos would understand.
Aren't we,
after all, centuries ahead of
Ovid and his recognizable
metamorphoses
(a fist into a railroad engine
like Jove into a swan)?
Almost anything worth
contemplating
is un-
explainable without distortion
(explained he,
didactically).

Workaday

It's Monday and it's
back to work. No more excuses.
The hanging plant
must've been at work
all night, hanging
practically to the floor—
while here, it's
sunny on the desk.
The sun is shining
with morning intent
like an instruction from
The I-Ching .
You don't need to read it
that way but I do, which
tells me something too.
Everything
is telling, and some things
are listening, including me.
I hear the faucet water
singing in one tone, and the more varied
Ravel piano composition.
Now the phone is ringing.
Someone
calling me from the world,
where work is needed—
industry, drive. How else
do you expect
the time to turn,
or to put needed things
on the table?

Poem in Favor of Cats

After a rain, the breeze is cool
and you get an old towel to
wipe the damp lawnchairs
because you want to sit in the presence of
dogs howling all over town at this
after-a-rain feeling that is infectious.
It infects you
but you don't want to take any pills for it.
The wind chimes ring and the cats
don't mind what you do, even if
you happen to be the meter reader
and what you do is predictable
(though not acceptable to the dogs).
Everywhere, the breeze
seems to be proclaiming freshness,
spirit-of-adventure, and this
irks the dogs, who don't like
the boat rocked, which is difficult
not to do after a rain—
the channels and arroyos gushing
with recent water that is
flushing debris downtown,
where it belongs, away from
residential backyards where cats lie
in the sunniest spots, basking,
and, as always, satisfied.

GRACE

You're lonely and can not learn
social graces because the people
keep going away to the marketplace.
Isn't it melancholic
how the sparrows chirp? And the wildroses
turn darker red, wilt, and slough their petals?
They'll be back next year, you hope,
but that's only generalized life, not
the individual (as all the best
religions keep emphasizing,
and you try to listen.)
You listen with a general ear
because the specifics are so narrow,
the one specific path for only
some, and no one very interesting.
Wanting only to be
certain makes even death
a bore. still,
each morning wakes you
at a new location, a composite, probably,
from what you know but didn't know
you knew, and what you don't know
seems new to you and keeps you
happy. Ah,
to be in the hands of something
with such craft
and imagination!

Overcast

I guess we'll be going soon.
We won't be staying here,
then, much longer,
where I hoped we could,
so I could melt into
the landscape—the profusion
of dark-red wildflowers near the
cinderblock wall, for instance.
Or the complicated repertoire
of the show-off bird in the morning
as you're contemplating
a second cup of coffee with milk that
pales against these
wild exuberances. Overcast
can push your equilibrium
over. Without even a free fall,
you can find yourself
flat on the sand,
not a dune near by to climb
in hopes of seeing the ocean—
because all the beauty of this region
receded, and it's nothing
but gravity now
that you must have to pull yourself up
against
by some cliché or other
if the sky ever hopes
to re-open, the sun to shine,
and your life re-dedicate
itself to something alert
or shiny.

By and Large

Beautiful sadness of the big city
in the evening that I like to
read about in Frank O'Hara.
stores that stay open "terribly late"
so you can imagine their glow
from your polished bus seat—just as
here,
the beautiful slow heat
that eventually saturates
every blade of grass
and irregular areas of earth between
the grass
(or is it "grasses"?)
All that really matters is
that you are here, that "really matters"
be used, the common phrase,
because we all are
common as the earth, not proper
as people want to seem,
where appearances is all that matters,
matter itself subordinated,
feelings masked.
Here
where yellow roses and brighter yellow
sunflowers in the yard
and mosquitos where you forgot to rub
some Off on
prick you alive.

Fire Ants

I don't need
the reading glasses.
I don't want distinctions
between the written
and the living page
on which grass is sparse
and you better
watch for goat heads.
They'll stab right through
your slippers as you
run across the yard trying to
scare that mocking bird
that won't shut up. He's
fixated on your yard and cats.
Beautiful wings won't
save him from the pump gun
pretty soon, I'm warning you—
despite the beautiful
restraint
practiced by the yogi Milarepa,
speaking to you
out of deep snow, his place
in the eleventh century.

CURRENTS

By now, the day's
freshness is sailing
over the Pacific Ocean.
I don't care. I have
my shady corner on the couch.
My book. I could
pick up the guitar
if I felt like
stretching. In fact, I do
look out the back
at the pristine diamond
pattern the afternoon sun
is engraving through the trellis.
Geometry used to give
the answers, you know.
One could still investigate that.
Or even if I'm not
so certain
of a particular word
or name of flower,
I know how sitting back
while listening
to the front porch wind chimes tinkle
feels.
It feels comforting.
The *ristra* of strung red chiles
swinging on the porch also
lets me know the breeze
is here,
having traveled from
who knows
how far.

GNARL

It's already reached the designation
"hot",
and me getting up
before the sun
so I could sip coffee in the dark
and think that the dream
of having to walk back home from
interstates away
would on-go, slowly,
me beside the highway
where weeds are not accustomed
to be looked at slowly and intently—
so that they practically shrivel
at the sight.

Evidently wanting hard
to return some where,
but unspecific,
the way you learn to seem
indifferent, so that no one
can catch your eye,
to insinuate.

Everything, apparently, is open, bright
with sunlight along every surface, airy
through the branches
so that the bird songs
carry. They can't belong to you,
of course, any more than the wide blue.
But underneath, or from inside,
is a reptilian craving.

If you stand around authoritarian, a phrase
leading to a phrase
until there's no air left
for the other
person's thoughts,
and in that way thinking you can
gloss your croaking in the dark,

it won't allow you, some time,
to hear the faintest
air
you never before thought
to listen for,
and that can swell
into a rich music.

DIALOGUE

I felt such a great isolation!

I stood outside myself
looking in through the window.

Cats played in the yard
inside their own fur.

I understood why I had to be who I was,
or, conversely,
how to become
whoever else—no,
                not quite true.

            You're confusing
            distance with freedom.

            You're not clay in your own hands.
            You were modeled
            after somebody else.

            You can't reach completely
            outside of yourself
            to turn yourself outside in.

I'm back in the back yard.

That frantic blob of life
at the tip of the apricot tree
turns into a finch.

The Cool Blue

Wednesday already, but the cool
still holding (thanks
to the breeze), as the blue
sky still holds us all
(thanks to God)—in which
a beautiful bird glides by
over my head,
though I'm not getting ahead.
But that kind of ambition
doesn't interest me
enough. It's the other
kind, without glasses,
that I love—
rugged, restrained (with a mountain
on top of it, as told
in the *I Ching*, and on top
of that, a lake.) We all
crossed the lake
in a small boat,
and in the shade of a grocery store,
awaited the bus that would
take us to the next world.
We could've talked
but chose, instead, to think
about hats, the sky
being so close, our heads
so much the center of things,
we might've been students
of Plato, peripatetically mute,
"international" in the sense of "between",
between one place and the next, the bus

on a boat on the lake
floating over the still waters
our way.

LAKEHEAD

If this is Sunday, the noises
must be of people rushing
to the park. A breeze comes
and goes through branches
above picnics,
or it'd be too hot
considering the charcoal grills
on which meat is sizzling and corn
cobs.
Get out the bats and gloves,
somebody in the position of
organizer,
or else set up
the nets, or put the trunks on
if this were Chicago
by the lake. The lake
that always plants its
wet kiss that grows into a flowering
memory that enfolds you
with its scent of deep
clammy water and you drown
inside it, it inside
you, into equilibrium
seculorum
and you don't get dry
even afterwards driving inland
or, actually, on the land
with its tendency to solidify
and thus draw a clean-cut line
between earth and sky
on which your head
is floating.

Morning Meditation #2
—Paisano Ranch, Texas

"Not me" is right. I'm not
a lot of things. For example,
here on this palatial lawn
with birds of all stripes singing
at me. Not even "at me", I'm sure.
They carry on
their love and warfare and I'm not
really here at all.
In this allegory, surprisingly, the birds
represent eternity. I, the foolish
mortal interloper. Whoops! Excuse
me! Did I just
drop in? Excuse my dust!—on this
lawn-carpet that extends forever
because green grass is simple enough
to keep recurring, each reincarnation
alike, maybe a new variety
of grass, but who would notice?
Whereas mortals seem to recur
each time more dwarfed
or selfish or any other
deadly sin.
Even the priests exhibit this
on their visages. Imagine
how the rest of us must look.
Better to grow a beard if
possible, which proves my
mother right, her "what are you
trying to hide" insinuations
that I ignored, being

young and hopeful.
Now, older and more honest,
I'm not really under this
moss-covered oak tree grown
from an acorn at all,
nor under this blue,
more pale because of the humidity,
which for the grass and trees
translates as rain, eternal cycle
of evaporation
and condensation
that Mr. Shordyke,
in 7th grade Science,
first taught us.

A Word

For weeks I've been
resisting letting life
happen to me, a small
orange cabin among the concrete
highrises in this city where
people frighten me with their
mother tongue—
people who walk unbuttoned
and swing their arms
to work, at times growling
inside their cars, where
one is not
allowed to know
their deepest
secret. Mostly,
we walk along,
grow tired in the heat,
stop to eat, buy, pay,
hardly need to use a word—
a word
that, after all, is only
the extension
of a gesture.

—Campinas, Brazil,
for David and Pam

Return Home

A mocking bird is
running through his
re-per-toire,
and, further out, a dove
coo-coos. In the pool
created by the waterhose
under the tree, black grackles
are alighting
for their bath.
The sky, milky,
makes me squint
but I don't mind my mind
being permitted to
turn slowly
as a cooling rotor on a roof,
its metallic cap gleaming
as it turns,
with slits
to air the mind.

Leaves

Left to your own
devices, with, of course, a little
raw material—such as the leaves,
who don't consider themselves
as such—and isn't that
being alive? The leaves
with their underside venation
and their chlorophyl,
who hang
around the mother tree all season.
Hardly a sigh or nasty word,
they shade you from the harshness
you'd sometimes
prefer—
so then you move
a branch or decide against
a cabin in the woods, its
cozy quality you
sometimes want. Want. Want
and it is yours, you feel—
whereas the leaves
await their turns.

GOD

is the memory of walking
with you on Sheridan Road,

discovering a new chain cafe,
maybe starbuck's.
Do they serve bagels at starbuck's?

We had stood
by the still waters
outside the Loyola library
talking—

where, as a freshman,
years earlier, I studied biology and math
for the exams, never learning
you had been born.

Now, you were with me.
I would not want.

That must be why
a vague reference to god
in a book I was reading
called out

to remind me to give thanks
for your goodness and mercy.

NAKED CHILDREN

Is it too late
to be children? If we wish
it? A pine scent
tickles our noses,
draws us into the shady woods
Hansel & Gretel-like—though,
so far, no witch.
Only strips
of sunlight filtering through,
and tree stumps where we stop to listen
for the mystery,
then, together, walk along the trail
that takes us to the hidden meadow.
Nobody can find us here,
except the black birds looking down
and cawing, which we hear as
laughter, nature reveling
in our naked pleasure,
lying on your sweater, my
Levi shirt, that we brought tied
around our waists just
for this purpose—
to give each other,
and receive, this joy,
en-joy each other,
children, naked in the woods.

Ripe Fruit

The last, dark, wildrose
bouquet of the season
blooms on its bough
over the cinderblock wall
near where a white butterfly
flutters, tasting and touching.
If it weren't for a neighbor's hammering,
it'd be tranquility
to get up into from breakfast
and explore
the ongoings in the grass
bounded by lattice and cinderblock wall
where wilted petals, splotches of shade,
and cats lie
side by side with streaks of
recognition.
You're getting old
and young women seem more
voluptuous fruit now
than when you, also voluptuous, hungered
for permanence—
as in that Japanese movie last night
where the repressed male
explodes
and finds himself in a backwater
of eels, weeds, and ordinary
human life, like his own—
voluptuous and seasonal.

Morning Meditation #3

—Paisano Ranch, Texas, for Bob & Lee

Take off your reading glasses,
why don't you? Then maybe
you could see the bigger picture—
which has always made me feel
guilty,
even right now,
probably my mother's influence,
her belief in altruism (a word
I couldn't even recall just now), despite
the fact she's selfish too:
thus understands me—
is actually speaking to herself—
though I get to keep her guilt.
Anyway, from here, the bigger
picture is green—trees,
grass, bushes—and a white-gray sky
stirring up a breeze that feels
ominous.
I was reading Eileen Myles' poems
romanticizing Manhattan where the weather
is an adornment
to the streets, buses, buildings,
whereas here, away from human culture,
you're at its mercy, forced to remember,
if you can't avoid it,
what urban human life
is still wrapped up in.
Now Lao Tzu
and other Eastern philosophies
make sense!

And "the victory of technology".
Even owning your own home
or, at least, having a decent apartment.
And having clothes, a hat
to protect you from "the elements".
Elementary, like the first
few grades—or was I just
younger then? and along
with me, the city?
the town? (which sounds much
friendlier, a nice old lady
watching out for you
out of her kitchen window).
The wind picks up. Bird songs
carry from inside the trees
as in a Tarzan movie, even
the ridiculously bright-red
cardinal expressing
a sense of ease
in there,
as the sky darkens.

At The Zoo

Orange, shaggy haired orangutan
with your sad bangs—
or sleek, white tiger,
pacing crazy—
or scared South American mouse, reflective
in your glassed-in house you share
with a papaya and a sloth
on Paisano street, El Paso—
it's cooler out here in the open air,
and when it heats up,
I go find shade.
Maybe there'll be rain, or
rain may decide to
wet another place
according to its free
enterprise—which you're not permitted
to enjoy, no choice
whether to listen
to the drinking fountain trickling
in its Greek-like base,
or to sit a moment
and enjoy similarities in people's faces
passing by, their eyes, and nice,
simple mechanism for walking
upright. See,
some things in nature just
occur—
don't always have
to be exotic,
and self-conscious.

5:45 P.M.

We're sitting here by ourselves.
The relative quiet. The light
down but not out. Birds
sometimes ("night hawks", according
to Grant, wheeling and diving
for bugs). Or else chrysanthemums
in thick little bouquets
in the yard
(is that the wrong way?) Cars
returning from downtown
parking lots outside offices, stores.
Where to come back to
but here, however meager?
No, that's excessive. "However plain."
Without the glamour, but also
without the veneer.
What is authentically ours.

Rooms

—for Roger

In the empty house, Ravel's
unobtrusive piano pieces
accompany me to the kitchen
where I run water
into the coffee mug
I place in the sink—

then through the house
of ordered rooms, each
room designed with a purpose.
Here, the room to lie
down in softness
with warm covers.
Here, the room to sit,
read, maybe gaze
out of the window.

In each room, furniture,
books, clothing, keepsakes
in set places—
usefully,
intimately.

STOMACH SLIGHTLY ACHING

You were always afraid—stomach
slightly aching—of not getting
respect, though now a stainless steel
chimney atop the neighbor's roof
stands out above the trees and the
discolored picket fence on which
grackles sometimes congregate or people
on either side stand face to face—
to face each other's ambiguities, I guess,
due to differences in facial
lines—each map a factor of
nervous system multiplied by life encounters.

The sun, which is also light, or fire,
penetrates through leaves and branches
to the ground—which is amorphous and
sometimes dark—in other words,
a complement.

           That's why, standing
on the ground, you seem
uncertain and waver like a sail
or any surface accessible to a breeze.
Here comes one now—from the west,
I think—though the actual air you feel
was always present, only more
perceptible now that it's set in motion,
like you like to move around, to avoid
stagnation, which nature abhors—though,
usually, it doesn't lose its temper.
And when it does, lawyers call it

"an act of God", unable
to believe that nature would act willfully,
as you would more confidently
come and go
in a world
more truly natural.

SQUARE IN THE DIAMOND

Square in the center of
a diamond opening in the
trellis is an orange
something.
It sways
slightly when the wind blows.
Just like a grackle screeches
slightly because the day is balmy and
milky overcast
as far as the sky's concerned,
which seems completely,
just like you seem everyman,
woman, and child. We all
have the same nervous system, don't we?
The same carpal bones in the wrist
to absorb the blow from
when we fall
and threaten to injure our ulna.
The birds on the powerline nod.
One bird unveils bright red
underwings as if to say, "It's magic
that we should be alive, thinking
our poems quietly unless
we happen to have opposable
thumbs to write with".
And the locust tree
continues growing
wrinkles in his bark
from stretching out
his limbs to us in solace
when the sun is bright,

though now the sun is blotted out
behind this milkiness
that allows the redness,
yellowness, and orangeness in the leaves
to truly shine.

THIRST

Can we please turn off
the sentimentality? All thoughts
can flow wherever they like
as long as it's not downhill
where there's a chance of a green valley.
Up here, high and dry, we're lucky
if the ratty grass has even a tinge
of green—though yellow
can be seen as austere and courageous
too. Meanwhile, the yellow-headed
sunflower-stalk slightly sways,
maybe toward the thorny
wildrose that lost its petals
earlier in the spring
when I felt less jaded, less
exterior. Inside yourself
is a richer vein, the possiblities more
organic and exploratory—
like anything dug up
raw and true. Ah, to feel
the feeling that you feel!

ALCHEMY

1.
So what
that it's afternoon
and I haven't
done something famous yet!
Gray thinks I better rub him
first, as a wind comes
blowing leaves down
that once were golden, especially
when illuminated
by the sun. Just like
in medieval days of alchemy,
except that now we know
the philosopher stone
is just a way of speaking.

2.
Gray trots off in the direction of
the bird sounds (which
to his ears must sound
like lunch).
The wind has stopped.
In fact, it's no longer after-
noon. The earth has
rotated. (And how was it
at the edge of
the abyss?) It's back
to morning now.
Blue sky is back.
Bright light.

Morning Meditation #4

I want so many things but mostly
what was 20 years ago
to be right now
because I'm 20 years too late
(formerly, it was 10 years)
and getting later.
The backyard mockingbird has
turned aggressive since I went away.
Now that I'm back, most
of the apricots ripened and fell
in my absence and it hailed
and rained and nearly tornadoed
though now it's clear and warm
soon-to-be hot, have to get up
early
to catch the worm (though
the mockingbird is even earlier).
Time makes me sick
even though supposedly it's
our creation, but that's how
society (us)
gets us (me)
to work—even retirees
evidently have to continue
fretting and regretting
if they want to collect
their pay.
Mostly I want
Kathleen Fraser still
to be her gentle,
photogenic self
(back cover of her book *New Shoes* ,
1977).

STATIC

Sometimes it's not sufficient
to sit
and, thus, to meditate.
Sometimes, though the periwinkles
be green and cheery
along the wall. And the plastic
lawn chair, color also green,
so as to seem
natural, though with lines too
regular to be designed
by what designed birds.
You're in your purple t-shirt
and sometimes you shiver
in the wind, like a Chinese
wind-shirt
or whatever
part of speech
you choose to speak
or chooses you.
It's Friday
to be among the birds and trees
except you're where the branch
dead ends.
Doves for loves
while the other people otherwise
make livings
out of money earned
or run
on their careers.

WHERE YOU END UP

The clouds keep moving
and as they pass under
the sun, they radiate
melancholy. I remember
a stomachache
after a girl had lost
interest in me—
which must have been
a "broken heart".
But you tend to lose
direction,
as when intuiting
where to turn left
because your neck feels
better on that side,
though that's not necessarily
where the road
turns up the hill
and out of a town
you'd rather
forget about anyway,
and over the
horizon that always
promises the ocean,
at the edge of which
you can lie and listen to
the waves chattering
in foreign accents,
from places far away.

Western Wind

Remember that medieval
English poem
in which the sailor
at sea longs
for "the small rain"
to sail him to his love
back home again?

I remember launching
poetry with that poem—
Intro To Lit, mostly Ed-
majors struggling
that first day to
demonstrate an interest
in those few
weird words.

So today, the wind
agitating on the porch:
ristra, wind chimes, junipers
alongside the house
thrash, jar my head
back
across that span again.

Mr. Chips

Will I ever live again
in semesters—as in the dream
where I had forgotten to buy
my textbook?
Late for class. Sunny. students
"milling around". What do the students
do when they stop milling?
I guess they pair off
and go down to the river (that is,
if the vista were pretty enough, easily
snappable, frameable, memorable).
All paths through the campus
criss-crossing eventually, which is
some kind of a metaphor
or pythagorean philosophy.
You can study both disciplines
in their respective departments, sit next to
your friend (who happens to be
female) on a plastic
chair they provide.
There's even a place
where the chair comes from, with forms
and a secretary.
It's set off from the student union,
the dorms, the football team
(who practice not
to notice the cheerleaders,
in case they should fall
or misspell a cheer).
Saturdays, classrooms
are empty, the walks strewn with leaves

and flower petals.
The shouts from the stadium
reverberate faintly from brick walls
and ornamental fountains
inscribed with long lists of
names from the past.

MISTER OCTOBER

This morning, the leaves having turned
to yellow saucers on the redbud, like melancholic flags,
I refuse to dwell on anything. The Cubs
are cellar-dwellers as it is,
and the Yankees won; my dead uncle
wouldn't be surprised.
Jill runs off to her mother's
to get a blanket for stan, who's visiting.
Junior, the plumber, assures me
that the rusty subterranean heating pipe
he replaced will not
be a conduit for roaches—though I can still
dream about it, can't I?
In last night's sequence, people parachuted
down on us, on cold rocky cliffs
overlooking the ocean. When I went to get my wife
to go back to our regular
home, all the women
were sleeping naked in a pile
on the kingsize bed.
So I went back to the men, who stood around
talking practical—such as:
pipes, valves, clamps,
that you gotta have
to heat the house.

Morning Meditation #5

So what's frank o'hara up to
40 years ago? (His expression's so
au courant). He lives "above a dyke bar"
and he's so happy. And I live
beside an apricot tree and beside
a bunch of regular joes (am
one myself) in small, unspectacular
city, usa, where one waters
the lawn on alternate days:
even or odd.
Even the odd tomcat
who talks back to one
is missing
and the yard is quieter
and infested with young, tender doves
now that said predator
is absentee.
And the apricots turn
orange, drop off the tree,
and become dessert.
And the stenchy gym shoes
from a river-trek
dry out hanging on the line
and are shoved far back
into the closet.
Oh but out of any drawer
may still emerge
the missing purple
t-shirt
that made one feel so

young and marlon brandoish!
(though faded now
while holding its tapered shape).

Birthday Poem

Ah, October,
the silence in the yard
under the locust tree
disrupted
by a power mower and Buddy next door
barking at a meter reader.
Only a few leaves
yellowing, one or two occasionally
falling on my hair or shoulder
as I sit beside the burning
citronella, probably ineffective
against mosquitos, but
why take a chance?
My stomach growls
from getting up too early.
If it were Saturday, I would buy some
honey from the pretty honey-lady
at the farmers market—
her hippie smile and business
acumen—because all of us
need to be "in business"
to "make a living" in America
(as if being alive
were insufficient, something
Buddhists also believe
and I can understand, but not appreciate,
that being born
is a mistake).
The citronella flame
gives off black smoke into the
pristine October atmosphere,
the far-reaching cloudless sky

against which our stunted southwest trees
are laughable, our realm
of earthly life being such a
narrow band between one
oblivion and another.

Pleasure Bay

The rowboats with their oarlocks
have rusted with old age
and petrified.
The trees turn so
deciduous in October
hardly anyone remembers
going rowing carefreely
with his father, grip
on the oar, bow
pointed toward the slushy
putrefaction—that
continues
to give pleasure,
the way the landscape of
word-fed traces
emerges
from between the cattails.

CLARITY

Amazing, how out of
nothing!

Of course, the chairs
are there

adding a certain
Kaiser *permanente.*

The cats
lie in between, or leap

all of a sudden in tall
October grass along the wall—

removed from which, air
arrives,

whose passage
the wind chimes
recollect.

STILL

Despite the millions of
times
from the past, there's still
right now.
Right now, where I'm beginning to
feel hungry,
but not just for a sandwich.
There's a whirring sound
of activity and I remember I'm in the city.
Can a city have intense sunlight?
Can people become interesting
and beautiful from getting hit
on the head by the sun?
Mythology said it could happen.
Ask a professor of mythology,
a mythological professor.
There's nothing logical
about it, and, therefore, not
impossible,
just as the sun can shed smells
as well as light—of brown pine needles,
for example, or sprinkler water
drying on the cinderblocks.
And later on, right now
will come again.
And so,
on.

SOLEDAD

Now
that the little white cat
has been dead,
and the other little white cat
who sniffed at the leaves,
and the gray tomcat
is scabbing, spending
most of his days asleep,
and nothing, practically,
that mattered
is still here (though new things
keep mattering, this year's
yellow flowers, for example,
under the peach tree)—
                    "so"
would seem to go well here, if I
were going somewhere
with this,
such as to the mountains
with Jill,
our yucca sticks wrapped in duct tape
to walk with and tap on
the rocks against snakes.
And jam in the crevices
to pole-vault us
into the quiet canyon of pink
liver-rocks
where there's a creek-vein
sometimes with water,
juniper trees in deep interstices
to watch over the place,

and in the rock face,
a cave
dark as a heart.

SAPPED

There's some green
in what you say, tree,
but mostly yellow,
pale,
translucent.
All over town, I
start to hear that
voice. November,
you're having a real effect.
I can't remember
when—clouds banding
and, after that, they'll
clump. The sun
won't show his face.
The gray, warped
back of the fence.
Same fence
my neighbor sees.
Not the same.

Sonata

The afternoon peels off
slowly. Like an onion.
Like a Ravel piano
contemplation (if one can
contemplate with one's fingertips).
Because the day that shows signs of
brightening was gloomy
for very long,
a powdering of snow
in mountain couloirs and on the edges—
and how else to live
but on the edge? One is never
midstream until after the fact,
in the after-thinking.

Yes, I've thought about it.

These days you wait
expectantly, being the holidays, but the mailman
brings the usual junk
(though we, of course,
appreciate every effort on our behalf).

And now it's later, the ivories
still touchingly
evanescent as the sunlight's
in and out. Out as the cat
who's getting cold despite
his fur,
like that thinskinned homeless man
last night at Hastings, chatting

with the clerk, his "comforter"
outside the door
a cold, thin bundle.

Not that I care enough
to "change my life" because of it,
to paraphrase Rilke.
                    Must be
that Rilke was younger.

Must be that it's getting colder.

Not "Depressed" Exactly

You can't will
a feeling
any more than rain
will come again
and turn the afternoon
dim and melancholy
like a
while ago
you whiled away
and now you're sorry
that it's gone.
Won't it come back?
Even if you plead with it?
The house feels
empty in this natural light
despite the paperbacks
colorfully along the wall
and a bright red
record cover.
But it's no use. Weather
knocks
when you're least
prepared to
drop what you considered
pressing.
Now you're left with
pangs
that don't add up.

In A Drizzle

—for Arthur Suarez, 1912-1998

By the time the blue
reaches here, this feeling
may be over, another
Ravel piano composition
playing—though the bronze llama
we found in a courtyard shop
in Cuzco
will continue
standing on the bookshelf
staring at the blank wall—
like a memory,
or when someone dies
and you can never
know them
in any fresher way.

When you were young, you hoped
to develop
friendships with whomever
came your way.
People might not be as simple
as you saw them,
just as language
might be grappled with to mean
more,
a kind of music,
or the clouds' endless
transformations—even when
it's drizzly gray, and rain

patters on the sidewalk
like happy voices.

Hope
is sky blue and has faith
in magic, like the sun
behind a drizzly day.
Death seems
like an exhaustion,
but may just be
a temporary
set.

CONFLUENCE

The book speaks
of "light lines" and "dark lines"
as I sit in the shade sun
breaks through the clouds
and I see
it's October when lines
of green grass yellow
though last night it was
raining coming
out of the restaurant and
we ran to our car
this morning the aluminum
rotor on the shed roof
turns the wind makes
the boughs sway for the cats
to jump at nature's alive.

December Song

Oh, December, you've
come again
with your brooding overcast
that is, however, temperate enough
to let me sit out of doors
(though I've had to cover the table
with plastic
against the wet).
Will you be
drizzling again very soon?
You inspire the wind chimes
to tinkle, and I interpret
this as an answer.
I'm probably just a failed
Catholic with ears to
heaven, after all,
despite being disillusioned in youth
in frozen Chicago
when I knelt in a cathedral
one afternoon
expecting thunder peals
to answer my adolescent demands—
walking out afterwards
covered in goosebumps and relishing
my deep ache, the city's squalor,
feeling my thighs
through my pockets, glad
to be walking alone
on Broadway, my slit eyes
providing a refuge for my
melancholy.

You're here again,
as you come every year,
with your dark humor
that soaks the tree trunks
black and rattles the bare limbs.
Your gray, low-lying clouds
glide over the landscape
bringing all things closer so that
I feel kinship
with the trees,
the pitiful, boxy houses,
the wet walking stick
leaning alone
against the cinderblock wall.

Sandstone Rock

—for Mike and Lisa

Perfectly sandstone rock, veined
like fine marble
or a marvelously exquisite
brown woman with veins—
you came
out of an isolated canyon
where the Navajos are
(though some Navajos are
ubiquitous),
to lie under a picnic table
in my back yard and look pretty,
whereas before, you were
functional, helping to hold up a cliff
in a canyon which in an earlier
geological time must've been
something else I don't know what
I never studied geology go look it up.
But you
were part of the "matter" then
that makes up the earth
that we walk on,
or skid down on, or pick at
with our fingers to take home
because we want so much to be
part of it—
our lives seeming so
insubstantial in contrast
whenever we take time
to stop.
Mostly we flash past, assuming

we're doing something
important. Never just being,
like you,
without questions, without caring
how you look. And you
look just fine—reddish brown grainy
sandstone with dark veins
running through, strata
of time
and convulsions,
that we only
can model
our art after.

Might Just Be

Some days (like today)
this might just be
a back yard, one cat on the ground
under your chair.
The Siamese other "king
of the mountain" (having won
the tabletop for a change).
Why are there
reddish, greenish, and yellowish
rocks on the table?
Why must you know?
The periwinkle climbs halfway
up the cinderblock wall, doesn't it?
Twenty years ago, who would've
thought it? Twenty years ago
the back alley would not
have considered itself part of the yard.
Things were less
like they are now
then. You, even, only beginning
to think as yourself.
Imagine! But let's
keep it within bounds.
Within this afternoon, bread
still needs to be baked,
catnaps completed
before the sunset turns cold,
gifts wrapped for children
who still need to arrive
to unwrap them.

In The Back

Just a momentary
aberration or a flash—and
the quiet
returns. So nice
of a breeze to come along,
and of a balance
of shade and light.
The white-pawed cat must be
a microcosm, as must
the leaves
with their two sides
to every argument,
though who can argue
with this plan?
I don't feel even slightly
confrontational, though I am
verging on hungry—
which must be the stomach's way
of entering
this conversation. You're right.
I let the mind
go on too long. Time
to re-new the flesh. Ah,
time! Such a great
reminder!

Colophon

Set in *Saks-Goudy* designed, of course, by
Frederic W. Goudy. Originally commissioned
as the exclusive type for Saks Fifth Avenue, it
was "unveiled" in a grand ceremony in 1934.
Mr. Goudy thought it "as good a type as I have
ever made, or can make." In 1939, his Deepdene
studio burned to the ground, destroying all the
matrices and drawings for Saks-Goudy. After
World War 11, the type house that held all of
the remaining foundry type went out of
business and the type was apparently junked
for its lead. It has not been available at all until
Richard Beatty created this recent digital version
by photographing Saks Fifth Avenue ads
from 1934-35 to find enough examples
of each letter to replicate the type.

Book design by J. Bryan

Joseph Somoza lives in Las Cruces, New Mexico
with his wife Jill. He quit teaching at New Mexico State
University a few years ago. Now he sits in his backyard
full-time, where he reads poetry and Eastern philosophy
books and writes while eavesdropping on the town
going about its business all around him.

photograph by Jill Somoza